The Miscarriage of Racial Justice

A Civil Rights Presidential Timeline

Derrick Newton

"I'm one of the 22 million Black victims of the Democrats. One of the 22 million Black victims of the Republicans and one of the 22 million Black victims of Americanism. And when I speak, I do not speak as a Democrat or a Republican, nor an American. I speak as a victim of America's so-called democracy. You and I have never seen democracy — all we've seen is hypocrisy."

Malcolm X

Contents

Prologue 7

The Day the Earth Stood Still in Disbelief 10

The Fight for Civil Rights from January 1953 to January 1961 22

The Man Who Watched the Twin Towers

Burn Across the Entire World 28

The Man Who Brought "The Audacity of Hope" 34

The Man Whose Racism Divided the Country Beyond Belief 49

Epilogue 65

References 68

Prologue

Back in 2016, after making it back to my dorm room at UC Santa Cruz, I reflected upon the intensive week as the presidential election took center stage with the entire world's attention on America. Donald Trump was competing against Hillary Clinton to become the 45th President of the United States. When I ponder over that cold, dark, and blistering night, I recall feeling something in the air that sent a chill down my spine. According to all the polls on mainstream media, Donald Trump had zero chances of winning the election against a seasoned politician and previous First Lady like Hillary Rodham Clinton, whose husband Bill Clinton was our 42nd President from 1993 to 2001. In fact, no one imagined that Donald Trump would have won against anyone. However, I gravely underestimated the American people on that fateful night of November 8th, 2016. I never expected that our country's 2016 election was about to topple the very establishment of our so-called democracy.

A shocking moment like that is hard to forget. I recall watching CNN and FOX NEWS closely and keeping up to date with all the media surrounding the election. In everybody's opinion, Hillary Clinton was set to become the next President of the United States by a landslide. This convinced me to let my guard down for the night and sleep, because what could possibly go wrong? Every poll in the country continuously predicted and reiterated that she would take the crown since she was supposedly backed by most Americans. After all, why wouldn't she be, judging by the alternative? Approximately 3 hours later, a noise broke out that sounded as though an atomic bomb had detonated across the entire campus. As I awoke abruptly, I realized that what I assumed were the sounds of people cheering and applauding, were instead sounds of their painful cries of distraught. While grappling with confusion, I hurriedly knocked on my roommate's door to ask, "Hey man, what just happened?" He solemnly replied, "You won't believe it… Trump is our new president." My mouth hit the floor instantly because no part of me would ever have been ready to receive such devastating news.

The following day, I walked to my Sociology class, only to find a note posted on the partition saying that all classes were canceled for the day. Another flyer on the bulletin mentioned there would be a "hug-in" in front of the bookstore. To my astonishment, the entire campus was either seated or standing in front of that bookstore, consoling each other over Hillary Clinton's loss. This motivated me to hurriedly rush to the off-campus liquor store and grab a bottle of Hennessy to help cope with the madness and defeat. Despite falling short of the majority, Donald Trump received 304 electoral votes compared to Clinton's 227, making him only the 5th President of the United States to take power. He received the majority in the Electoral College despite losing the popular vote. This earth-shattering experience reinforced my contemplation on whether President Obama's election was responsible for Donald Trump's successful win. A Black man achieved America's highest position as Commander-In-Chief back in 2008 and served not one, but two consecutive terms. It is my genuine belief that White Americans were not ready for this, and even many Black Americans were in absolute shock when Barack Obama was elected as the nation's 44th president. Was Donald Trump's 2016 election white supremacy's way of correcting the so-called "wrong" that numerous people felt was a travesty and constitutional debacle putting African Americans in the highest position of the land? Considering recent events involving police brutality, has America's deepest, darkest, and racist roots been exposed on such a grand scale for the greater good? Or should we expect another shock in November 2020?

The Day the Earth Stood Still in Disbelief

Donald J Trump did not win the 2016 Presidential Election in the United States of America by a landslide. This victory was a challenging pill to swallow for many people around the world as despair set in. Little did people know that the four years following his triumphant win would be some of the most challenging times ever experienced. However, it is essential to identify who benefited from his election—and who perished because of it.

This book is a comprehensive overview of the most notable events preceding Donald Trump's victorious acceptance speech in 2016, and how the 45th President of the United States has changed the world we once knew.

The first thought that readers should contemplate is whether racism played a significant role during the elections and if there is a risk of history repeating itself again in 2020. Were white Americans jubilant about his victory due to their hatred resulting from enduring eight years of President Obama's government? Did African Americans believe that President Barack Obama should have upended all the unjust systems in place that empowered and cemented the systemic racial inequality millions of people continue suffering from? And finally, has the 45th president redefined the meaning of the United States of America by bringing the nation together to fight against his policies?

The most defining trait when it comes to the Trump era's national and foreign policies is confusion. This does not refer solely to the frequent gaps between the president and his administration's paths, but also to their morass of contradictions and his irrational personal decision-making impulses. No other president in the United States history has been as vocal as Trump to air their business to the world via online and offline media channels, namely Twitter.

The moment Donald Trump continued to use Twitter as his central platform to spread opinions after his election and rile up the citizens of this country is the moment that the most trouble began. It is beyond belief to witness how a man could single-handedly crash entire world economies or start global wars based on a single tweet by using a platform also famous for promoting humorous memes for comedic relief. Most people underestimated the lengths the president and his family would go to advance their own power at the expense of the American people, and now there is no stone left unturned as the entire world has experienced the tragic events that will forever go down in history to mark this administration's woes. The man who had spent eight years criticizing and deconstructing all of President Obama's policies somehow became the most powerful individual in the world, and this led to all the terror and confusion.

How can the same person who belittled Hillary Clinton for sending emails through a private server not be held accountable for colluding with foreign states who openly brag about their anti-American senti-ments? The man once threatened "fire and fury" against North Korea, only to later claim to have "fallen in love" with Kim Jong-Un, despite receiving no promises from the foreign country regarding whether they would keep their end of the deal by dismantling their nuclear arsenal. Donald Trump has always been reluctant to publicly criticize Vladimir Putin, and this enforced suspicions that his administration is closely influenced by the Kremlin.

The 45th President of the United States has always evidently trusted his own gut instincts over any advice from US officials for establish-ing local and international policies. Those very instincts have famously attracted him towards autocrats, while straying from traditional demo-cratic allies, in both the United States and abroad. This leads to another constant in the Trumpian approach, which is his drive to erase the leg-acy of Barack Obama and all his other predecessors. According to The Guardian, "Almost everything Obama was for, Trump has been over-whelmingly against, from the 2015 nuclear deal with Iran to trade deals in the Pacific or with Europe, or the Paris climate accord."

Prior to COVID-19, unemployment levels in the United States have been on a continuous downturn since man first landed on the moon. However, it is dubious for a president to take credit for "creating" employment, especially when most citizens are still struggling to make ends meet despite having multiple minimum wage jobs. Even though Donald Trump made a bold promise of "being the greatest jobs president that God ever created," he has emboldened racial hatred across the nation, and African Americans are paying the price for it with their lives.

Under the guise of Operation Patriarchy, old white men are relentlessly fighting an uphill battle against the changing demographics of this country. The 72-year-old president, along with Senate leader Mitch McConnell, are putting their best foot forward to safeguard white men's supremacy in all the high positions that control this nation. In the first two years following the election, they packed the courts with judges who are predominantly white, male, and conservative. The lifetime appointments of these judges mean that the federal benches do not visibly represent the entire country by excluding African Americans from rising to the highest levels of government.

This has been business as usual for Mitch McConnell since it has always been his go-to strategy. He steadfastly blocked dozens of Obama's nominees for federal courts by refusing to hold Senate votes. It was his major gamble predicting that in 2016, a Republican would win the presidency to support the appointment of more conservative judges. After supreme court justice Antonin Scalia's death in 2016, McConnell used his power over the Senate to hold that seat vacant for 293 days while refusing a hearing for Merrick Garland, who was nominated by Obama. Several white evangelical Christians felt that the vacant supreme court seat was one of the most compelling reasons to vote for Trump, even though he is a thrice married, alleged sexual deviant, who repeatedly boasts about assaulting women. It was no coincidence that after Trump won the presidency, a conservative named Neil Gorsuch was given the top job in the supreme court, followed by the dramatic assignment of Brett Kavanaugh. The latter was also embroiled in several sexual assault allegations.

Both McConnell and Trump have been racing to shift the district courts to a far-right spectrum. This was done at a much faster pace to undermine Obama's legacy while emboldening disgruntled white supremacists in the United States. The steadfast move provided white supremacists with a sense of security to feel like they are the "master race" and that everybody else is beneath them. This racism shone brightly under the spotlight and led to global condemnation and sustained bipartisan criticism both locally and internationally for Donald Trump, especially when the immigration ban was announced. It proved that the 45th president has no limits to how much suffering immigrants would endure for his own political gain.

For several months in 2018, the Trump administration forcibly separated migrants from their families, which provoked scenes of desperation in detention centers and border courtrooms as people begged and pleaded to be reunited safely with loved ones after the treacherous journey they endured to settle in America. Since 2017, thousands of children have been separated from their parents and caged in unsanitary conditions. This event escalated so brutally that even his favorite daughter and senior advisor, Ivanka Trump, described those months as "a low point" for the Trump administration. Despite calls for these racist policies to be abandoned, the administration kept doing a complete U-turn to pursue their extremist agenda. Part of their agenda is to silence people of color so that they always accept the status quo instead of fighting against it to achieve justice and racial equality. The incredible and powerful social movement, "Black Lives Matter," has taken over the world by storm following the deaths of George Floyd, Breonna Taylor, Elijah McClain, and many others. These murders exposed the extent of police brutality in the United States and how law enforcement officials endanger lives to protect the status quo of white privilege. The majority of the country has acknowledged that protestors' frustrations are warranted, and many top corporate names have also shown their support for the movement.

NASCAR ruled that fans can no longer fly Confederate flags at their races, and even the Pentagon and a small number of Republican senators are considering renaming military bases that honored Confederate soldiers. Corporate America has taken a bold stance against racial injustice, even if it is just on paper, whereas the Commander in Chief himself has not provided his support yet. The president increasingly sounds more and more detached and unphased by the concerns of the affected communities. He is the glaring outlier amongst the most cautious institutions and leaders finally beginning to talk openly about discrimination and reconciliation.

This should not come as a surprise, though, considering that the current sitting president has had a long history of making crude, tone-deaf, and insensitive racist remarks. While hunkering down at the White House, he continues to remain isolated with this dominant political and social movement, while tweeting conspiracy theories about injured soldiers and calling peaceful protestors "thugs." His use of this violent and harsh language is unlike anything seen before from other American leaders, and his words are often supported by white nationalists and defenders of white supremacy. Instead of supporting and praising the Black Lives Matter movement to appeal to voters who will be marching to the polls in 2020, he has sided with his own ignorance. Mayor Levar Stoney of Richmond, VA, said, "He's talking as if this is a country in the 1950s and not 2020," during a time when protesters rushed to topple Confederate statues — for good reason. These statues are a constant reminder of racial inequality through which white supremacists and slave owners were celebrated, thus hindering any progress towards achieving equality.

Currently, the country is confronting three overlapping crises: the economic collapse, the coronavirus pandemic, and a powerful reckoning with injustice and racism. President Trump's inability to show an ounce of empathy has illustrated how limited his political arsenal is. This is why people believe that the president does not want equality after all, because white supremacy is at grave risk, and that seems more important to uphold even though it is high time that the world advanced past racism. It also makes a person wonder how much hatred white nationalists have held for the last eight years when they had to endure an outspoken, compassionate, smart, humorous, and highly qualified president who is also a person of color. President Obama gave hope to the African American communities by showing that they, too, can rise above and achieve greatness despite being underappreciated and overlooked at every opportunity. However, he was not entirely a frontrunner for tearing down platforms of systemic racism because he acted more like a president, rather than an activist and advocate for minorities. Despite this, the blame could not be put on him entirely, as it was his job to perform as a presidential guardian for all citizens, even though all lives have never been equal from the start. Barack Obama did his best to show compassion and empathy, which is a quality still yet to be seen from President Trump, who is nearly at the end of his first term of four years in November 2020. If these four years were not enough for him to understand and empathize with the struggles African Americans face daily, a second-term win will only make things worse by further emboldening the wrong side.

The people continuously reinforcing Trump's decisions and instincts are advisors with their own agendas for crushing the Black Lives Matter movement. They purposely held a campaign rally on June 19th in Tulsa on the very day dedicated to honoring Black emancipation, also known as "Juneteenth." The city where the rally was held had seen the worst times of racial violence in the entire country's history over a century ago. The rally was not to support Black Lives Matter or the African American communities; it was held to criticize civil rights protestors of 2020 and mock their strides. For example, it is difficult to overlook the racial insensitivity when the president's very own campaign was promoting "Baby Lives Matter" clothing on its website at the same time protests against police brutality were being held across the globe. This was purposely done to mock BLM by replacing the word "Black" with any other word in order to undermine and distract from the focus of the movement. It is one thing to publicly hold back support for a movement that challenges white supremacy, but it is entirely unnecessary to attack BLM when citizens of America are in pain. In response to people's pleas to defund the police in the wake of racial brutality and injustice, Trump twisted the true goal of the movement to defund the police and said, "I heard they want to close up all police forces. It is not like they want to sort of bring a little money into something else. They want it actually closed. I am thinking, what happens late at night when you make that call to 911, and there is nobody there?" This remark gained plenty of applause from his supporters even though his words aimed to gaslight people. Defunding the police does not mean getting rid of them altogether. It simply means reducing their inflated budgets and allocating the funds to oft neglected yet crucial areas, such as housing, public health, and youth services. Still, it is also the very definition of fearmongering and gaslighting during a sensitive period where American citizens are grappling with the brutality of police violence towards minorities. The president is also going off on his own tangent away from Republican leaders. Even Mitch McConnell, the Senate majority leader, surprisingly praised the BLM protests by calling recent events "the obvious racial discrimination that we have seen on full display on our television screens." Whether this statement would lead to real action to curb racial inequality is yet to be seen, and only when there is real action will Black Americans feel safe in their country.

An overwhelming number of Republican voters and independents believe that George Floyd's murder in May represents a broader problem for policing. Bishop Harry Jackson, a black pastor who is one of President Trump's evangelical advisors, said, "We need to have this president and both parties say that 'We feel your pain.' There needs to be a discussion to African Americans and other minorities that the loss of life historically matters. Everybody has to feel that from him." This seems to have fallen on deaf ears because politically speaking, Trump has visibly aligned himself with cultural traditionalists and law enforcement officials, while remaining hostile towards the protestors. Rather than addressing racial inequality, he called protestors "looters" and "extremists," while praising law enforcement officers as "good people."

In a Washington Post-Schar School Survey, only 40% of Republicans over the age of 50 believed that killing George Floyd reflected a broader problem. In contrast, the majority of younger Republicans are appalled by police violence against African Americans. Wesley Donehue, a GOP strategist, based in South Carolina, said, "Younger Republicans want to see racial disparities fixed. If Republicans do not address these issues now, we will lose the next generation of young voters, just as we have [lost the votes of] minorities." This shows that the president is indeed concerned about his re-election prospects, but he has not won the crucial voters over and there is hardly any time left until the upcoming election. He has repeatedly stilted during these intense discussions while harboring offensive stances on race for many years, such as his searing attack towards The Central Park Five and his infamous suggestion that TV show, "The Apprentice," should have an all-White team competing against an all-Black team. Although America is currently grabbing white people's faces and saying "look, this is what is happening and you should not turn away," the most influential person in America is averting his gaze and emboldening white supremacists – the same people who are trying to undermine Black Lives Matter with "All Lives Matter." At the end of the day, the facts speak for themselves. All lives will never matter unless Black lives matter because racial inequality across the nation is glaringly apparent and tilted to one side. At the same time, the rest can continue enjoying their privilege.

As protestors are risking their lives to demand reforms, the president bizarrely believes that a strong economy is the best plan for tackling racial inequality. According to The Washington Post, Trump clarified that his priority is a strong economy, which is not the primary focus of Black Lives Matter. Impassioned protesters across the world are loudly demanding a complete overhaul of courts, institutions, and police departments. Meanwhile, he is ignoring all that to hyper-focus on the economy. When asked about his plan to address police brutality and systemic racism, he said, "It is the greatest thing that can happen for race relations, for the African American community, for the Asian American, for the Hispanic American community, for women, for everything, because our country is so strong. And that is what my plan is: We are going to have the strongest economy in the world." In bewilderment, many people wondered how a strong economy would end violence and racial segregation that still exists in many systems driving the modern world. The answer above reflected Trump's belief in the power of economic growth as the magical solution to every national ill, even though the unemployment rate is significantly higher for African Americans and other people of color. Instead of embracing the fundamental reforms demanded by protestors, his focus is echoing "All Lives Matter" without providing urgent support to African Americans so they too can be on a level playing field to enjoy any economic growth. A better economy will not bring justice to the families of those who have been killed at the hands of corrupt law enforcement officials, nor will it protect others in the future from facing the same hardcore brutality because of their skin color. To empathize with the victims, one must understand how Black Lives Matter came about and why it is the most critical movement of our lives that everybody needs to pay attention to instead of dismissing it by chanting "All Lives Matter." The people of America should stop ignoring and denying the fact that one group has always undergone the worst miscarriage of justice in this country.

The Fight for Civil Rights from January 1953 to January 1961

Dwight D. Eisenhower, the 34th President of the United States, or Dwight David "Ike" Eisenhower was not brought up to have sufficient knowledge and exposure to racism. He was raised in rural Kansas and had no African American teachers or friends growing up. Then his career led to a segregated U.S. Army where he served as a general and surrounded himself in white privilege with friends from the Old South while unwinding at Augusta National Golf Club.

The Age of Eisenhower

During his 1952 election campaign, Eisenhower declared his unalterable support of equality and fairness to all American citizens. On a federal level, Ike championed rapid desegregation in Washington, D.C, the nation's capital and followed through on Truman's momentum of desegregating the US army. According to an excerpt from the book The Age of Eisenhower: America and the World in the 1950s" by William I.

Hitchcock, "In 1953, he was putting pressure on the armed services to root out the last vestiges of segregation. Eisenhower announced the creation of the Committee on Government Contracts, a body designed to oversee nondiscrimination policies in the allocation of federal contracts. It marked a definite reversal for the president." Eisenhower also appointed Governor Earl Warren as his Chief of Justice of the Supreme Court in 1953. Warren had thrice won the California governorship and was a GOP vice-presidential candidate who classed himself as a moderate with integrity. Warren was Eisenhower's competitor during the 1952 presidential nomination and was later appointed to the top vacancy at the Supreme Court. This led to the court's overturn of the 1896 case of "Plessy vs. Ferguson," where states were permitted to segregate public venues and facilities according to race. The aim was to establish equal facilities and access for Black people, and Warren himself said that he was "separate but equal," and that inequality among races was against the Fourteenth Amendment of the Constitution.

This significant decision in history led to a lot of tension over the years, where all-white establishments grappled with the new legal demand to racially integrate their customers. Although some establishments such as schools readily complied with this landmark movement, other public schools shut down to avoid "race mixing." Southern members of Congress in 1956 challenged the Supreme Court's decision stating that it was an abuse of power, describing the situation as "having destroyed in a stroke the amicable relations between white and Negro races that have been created through 90 years of patient effort by the good people of both races." They wanted to denounce any agitators or dreamers who dared to bring revolutionary changes to the country, and they tirelessly fought to stop implementing desegregation in schools. The document used for denouncing the Supreme Court's decision was signed by 19 Senators and 82 Representatives. These people represented approximately a fifth of Congress. This proved that several people always accustomed to privilege did not want to shatter the status quo because they viewed equality as a form of their own oppression. Their resentment and opposition against Black Americans joining their ranks ran deeper than ever.

Although Eisenhower was providing hope to those desperate for change, he did not want to be a civil rights crusader. He often said in private that Black activists were selfishly demanding too much change in a short amount of time. However, he also refused to allow local schools and politicians to defy the Supreme Court's historic ruling. In September 1957, Eisenhower swiftly moved to prevent a school board in Little Rock from aiding a segregationist Governor and the Arkansas National Guard, who were motivated to bar African American students from attending White schools. He famously ordered units to take over the school to protect and assist Black students entering the building, despite the angry mobs shouting in the background.

Modern scholars believe that Eisenhower could have done more to express his support for the moral cause of equality and justice for all after the Little Rock incident, but his view on the matter was narrow. He did not champion the need for fairness and equality in America enough and called the angry Southerners "people of good will united in their efforts to preserve and respect the law." This statement closely echoes

Donald Trump referring to white supremacists at the Charlottesville alt-right protests during his first year in office as "very fine people," even though a 32-year-old woman named Heather Heyer was killed by them. Like Eisenhower, he half-heartedly condemns racism while also suggesting that both sides should be "equally" blamed. This is what made Joe Biden, the 2020 Democratic Presidential Nominee, claim that "Trump assigned a moral equivalence between those spreading hate and those with the courage to stand against it. And in that moment, I knew the threat to this nation was unlike any I had ever seen in my lifetime."

The Murder of Emmett Till

On August 28, 1955, while visiting family in Mississippi, a 14-year-old young African American named Emmett Louis Till was brutally murdered for allegedly "flirting" with a White woman. The White woman's husband and brother forced Till to carry a cotton-gin fan weighing 75-pounds to the Tallahatchie River. They ordered him to undress and then beat him half to death. Then they gouged his eye out before shooting him in the head and throwing his body tied to the fan with barbed wire into the river. Till had grown up in a working-class neighborhood in south Chicago. Even though he studied at a segregated elementary school, nothing would have prepared him for the brutal racism he tragically encountered in Mississippi. His family members warned him about taking extra care due to his skin color. However, being a young teenage boy like any other, he was bound to goof around a little, especially in harmless ways entirely normal for a White boy of the same age.

Four days before his murder, Till socialized with his friends and cousins outside a small store in Money and bragged to them about his girlfriend in Chicago being White. His companions did not believe him and challenged him to ask a White woman sitting behind the shop out on a date. This was only a friendly banter between friends and family members. As he exited the shop, he simply said, "Bye, baby" to the White woman named Carolyn Bryant. Since there were no other witnesses at the store, the woman running the counter said that he grabbed her and made lewd advances while wolf-whistling. When her husband, Rob Bryant, the proprietor of the store returned after a business trip and heard how Till supposedly disrespected his wife, he was enraged and stormed over to Till's great uncle's home with his half-brother in the early hours of August 28th. They angrily demanded to confront the boy, despite desperate pleas of forgiveness from Till's great uncle Mose Wright, and forced the child into their car. After driving Till throughout the night and possibly beating him senselessly in a tool house behind Bryant's half-brother's residence, they finally drove him down to Tallahatchie River, which was the final scene of the crime. Till's body was disfigured so badly that even though his corpse was recovered three days later, his great uncle could only identify him because of an initialed ring the boy wore. The brutality of this incident was beyond unforgiveable and the authorities in Mississippi wanted to bury the body immediately to cover their tracks. However, Till's grieving mother, Mamie Bradley, insisted that it be sent back to Chicago. Despite the poor child's body being mutilated beyond belief, Bradley held an open-casket funeral so that the whole world could see how those racist murderers killed her son.

When an African American magazine called Jet published the photo of Till's corpse, the mainstream media picked up the story, which led to Bryant and Milam going to trial in a segregated courthouse. Unfortunately, on September 23, an all-White jury in that segregated courtroom decided in less than an hour that Till's murderers deserved the verdict of "Not Guilty." This outraged people across the country who felt let down by the system that encouraged such violent hatred. The state's decision also did not charge the racist murderers with kidnapping either. However, The Emmett Till murder trial brought the world's attention to the segregation in the South and the brutality of Jim Crow, which became the early impetus of the African-American Civil Rights Movement. According to Tim Tyson, the author of "The Blood of Emmett Till," Carolyn Bryant later recanted her testimony and admitted that the young boy had never threatened or harassed her. She said, "Nothing that boy did could ever justify what happened to him," but it was too late. Her racist actions caused great suffering to an innocent American family, thus gravely upending their lives forever.

The Man Who Watched the Twin Towers Burn Across the Entire World

According to an article published by *Politico* on February 2020, "George W. Bush, the 43rd President of the United States, laments shocking failure in the treatment of Black Americans and expressed support for protests that have taken place around the world while denouncing looting and violence." This all sounds well and good in 2020, but history speaks for itself.

The Age of Bush

George W. Bush, the 43rd President who led America through one of the worst disasters in 2001 when the Twin Towers were struck by terrorists, had a complicated racial legacy despite acting as a modern-day ally. He was lauded as a decorous and courageous leader and described himself as a loving father with an appreciation for the zany parts of life.

However, his political strides to win the election were based on matters of race and equality. His strategy echoed subtle stereotyping, which played on people's fear, suspicion, and guilt. This is such a potent combination that inspired present-day Democrats and Republicans to emulate while reaching out to the public. Some African Americans and his political opponents believed that the Bush legacy demonstrated how pernicious allusions to race influence elections, followed by the consequences of exclusion and power. In 1988, Bush had an adamant stance on crime and cited an ad about a man named Willie Horton during his speeches to justify his opinions. This birthed modern racial politics and motivated Republicans to use the same tactics to maintain the status quo. He tried to pander to the Republicans who were, and still are, a predominantly white group. Leah Wright Rigueur from the Harvard Kennedy School of Government said, "What is much easier to do is say that this person is good or this person is bad when the reality is much more complex. What I have concluded is that Bush was a person who took a utilitarian approach to achieving power."

On his campaign trail, Bush frequently mentioned Horton as a specter of violence and uncontrolled crime. Tali Mandelberg, a political professor at Princeton and director of the Program on Inequality at the university's Mamdouha S. Bobst Center for Peace and Justice, said in the book *The Race Card* that "Bush himself repeatedly talked about Horton, an African American prisoner, so much so that he made him a household name." This was intentional so voters would associate Horton, a convicted criminal who raped and killed a White woman, with their racist fear of all Black Americans rather than only the individual responsible for the horrific crime. This resembles modern-day mainstream media where African Americans are plurally called "thugs" and "murderers." Meanwhile, White criminals such as Dylann Roof, who murdered nine parishioners at an African American church in South Carolina, are known as "lone wolves," which sounds less harsh despite the gravity of the crime. However, Bush was incredibly careful not to sound too racist to Black voters and knew that overtly racist messaging would turn off several White voters. His speeches about Horton did not resonate as racism right away, except for African Americans.

Bush did several good things to improve the country, such as signing bills passed by Democratic-controlled Congress to create urgent funding for healthcare even though he vocally criticized people suffering from AIDS and HIV. Bush also signed the Americans With Disabilities Act that made the country more accessible for those with disabilities. He even elevated a four-star general and firm supporter of diversity named Colin Powell to oversee inclusion efforts on war matters. However, he also nominated Clarence Thomas as head of the Supreme Court, who was woefully against the Civil Rights Movement. The 43rd president also vetoed the 1990 Civil Rights Act and gave a speech about the 1992 Los Angeles riots, which heavily implied that Black Americans deserve to be continuously monitored as though they are solely responsible for every crime in America. Armstrong Williams, a Black Republican and GOP politician who was still supportive of Bush's drive to gain votes from the Democratic Party, said, "There are no perfect men among us. If there ever were, they are either in heaven or dead."

The Shooting of Tamir Rice

Tamir Rice was a young and happy-go-lucky African American child throwing snowballs and playing with a toy pellet gun in Cleveland Park, when a White police officer named Timothy Loehmann shot and murdered the 12-year-old within seconds of getting out of his car on November 22, 2014. What started as a friendly game among children suddenly took a turn for the worst. Rice had gone out to the snowy park with a toy gun that many children owned that playfully fired plastic pellets from before he threw snowballs and settled down at a picnic table. He later tucked the "gun" away and walked to the edge of a gazebo as the squad car barreled across the lawn, and the officer ended the boy's young life within moments with no hesitation. As Rice lay dying and bleeding out from Loehmann's bullet, one officer in the car radioed saying, "Shots fired, male down. Black male, maybe 20, black revolver, black handgun by him. Send E.M.S. this way, and a roadblock." The boy was only twelve and had a child's playful pistol. When the county sheriff's office reviewed the shooting and released the security footage during interviews, they revealed several tactical errors and miscommunications that exposed institutional failures by the Cleveland Police Department that led to the murder of an innocent child whose only "mistake" was going outside to play in the park. Rice was shot in the abdomen at point-blank, which debunked the responsible officer's claims of "self-defense" and that he tried to warn the boy three times to raise his hands. When Rice's 14-year-old sister ran to the scene of the crime, the White officers aggressively tackled her to the ground and handcuffed her, even though she too was a child. When their distraught mother joined the scene, the White officers threatened to arrest her as well. While Rice remained on the ground taking his final breaths, officers Loehmann and Garmback did not bother checking any vital signs, nor did they perform first aid after shooting him from such a close range.

Two weeks after Rice's murder, the Justice Department released a horrific report accusing the Cleveland Division of Police of an ongoing pattern of excessive force, especially where officers were rarely ever disciplined. They also had suspicious hiring policies for recruits, with an inferior vetting process. Police records showed that the responsible officer Loehmann was given the job without any reviews from his previous department, from which he had resigned after suffering from a "dangerous loss of composure" during firearms training. Rice's mother had always been aware of racial inequality and prevented her children from owning a toy or water gun in case it was ever mistaken for a real one. However, Rice was a goofy child who wanted to hold a friend's airsoft pistol as any curious kid that age would, and he seemed delighted by the toy without knowing it would be the unfortunate cause of his unprovoked and untimely demise.

The Shooting of Oscar Grant

Oscar Grant III was killed in the early hours of New Year's Day in 2009 by Bay Area Rapid Transit Police Officer Johannes Mehserle in Oakland. A second officer, Anthony Pirone, aggressively kneed Grant in the head and forced him to lie down on the platform while holding him down in a prone position. Mehserle then pulled out his pistol and unnecessarily shot Grant in the back. Many videos captured on cell phones went viral across the media, leading to peaceful and violent protests. Grant was on the train when he got into a fight with another passenger. Although Grant's girlfriend and other passengers successfully deescalated the situation by breaking the fight up, the train conductor announced that the police had been notified and were waiting at the next station. The police picked people who they believed were involved in the fight, despite not witnessing it themselves. Officer Pirone approached two African American men and ripped one of their jackets off. Pirone saw that Grant was dressed in a similar outfit as the people sitting against the platform wall. He then removed Grant from the train before Mehserle abruptly stole his life. During an internal investigation, Pirone lied when he said he confirmed with the train conductor that the men he targeted had been involved in the fight. The train operator told Pirone she was unsure about the detained men, and that the police were simply guessing who was involved or not.

Grant raised his hands while he sat against the platform wall. Footage from cell cameras showed the court that Pirone stood over Grant yelling abusive profanities and using the N-word. As dozens of people watched while cursing the officers, Mehserle and Pirone knelt on Grant's neck and told him he was under arrest for resisting an officer, even though he was face-down and could not move. Then Mehserle attempted to handcuff Grant but could not reach his hands. Therefore, he abruptly unholstered his gun and fired into Grant's back. The bullet ricocheted off the concrete platform and pierced through Grant's lung. Grant was pronounced dead seven hours later at Highland Hospital.

The Man Who Brought
"The Audacity of Hope"

History was made on November 4th, 2008, when Barack Hussein Obama II, the first African American to serve in office, was elected as the 44th president of the United States (2009-2017). The world was in disbelief, and many tears of joy were shed not only across the nation but also the entire globe. This election meant so much to millions of people because they could finally see a reflection of themselves at the highest position the country had to offer.

The Age of Obama

Obama often described his own struggles reconciling with social perceptions of his multiracial heritage. He said, "I noticed that there was nobody like me in the Sears Roebuck Christmas catalog and that Santa was a white man. I went into the bathroom and stood in front of the mirror with all my senses and limbs seemingly intact, looking as I had always looked, and wondered if something was wrong with me." These words powerfully resonated with African American communities across the nation because he was finally giving them a voice they never had before. Before his election, many people often tiptoed around the topic of racial inequality and hesitated to shake the status quo, fearful that they may disrupt their careers and lives by doing so. Obama's inauguration took place on January 20, 2009. This was the day he inherited a global economic recession that brought millions of people to their knees during the housing market crash. He also had to deal with two ongoing foreign wars, while championing an ambitious financial reform, and pushed the narrative towards reinventing alternative energy, education, and healthcare as he lowered the national debt. These matters were essential to him and everybody in Black communities because they are intertwined with people's economic well-being. In his inauguration speech, Obama said, "Today I say to you that the challenges we face are real. They are serious, and they are many. They will not be met easily or in a short span of time. But know this, America, they will be met." This was the quote that gave people hope and belief that he was the right person to finally tear down the systems that led to racism so they could experience true equality for the first time in history.

Aside from showing the world what an eloquent, humorous, and compassionate man he is with the country's best interests at heart, he also tracked down the infamous al-Qaeda leader, Osama Bin Laden, who masterminded the 9/11 terrorist attacks. Obama's intelligent covert operation impressed the world because he organized an elite team of US Navy SEALs to raid Bin Laden's compound in Pakistan, thus killing him in less than an hour without causing any American casualties. Many believe this jaw-dropping event ultimately secured his second-term win. When he won against his Republican opponent Mitt Romney to serve another 4 years in 2012, he again addressed the nation and brought attention towards urgent issues, like marriage equality, healthcare, and climate change. However, in November 2014, Obama had to face numerous hurdles to get his policies across because the Republicans voted in large swathes to gain the Senate majority. This meant that he had to contend with an opposition party that controlled both houses of Congress during his final two years in office, and they went out of their way to block many of his progressive ideas. Although Obama was a beacon of hope to those who believed that their voices and rights would be heard, he acted more like a president and politician rather than an activist. This was not his fault, because he was elected to represent all Americans without showing favoritism to one race or the other. Congress voting against him at every stage also did not help either. He had a monumental task of trying to please every single person, and that is never possible. In turn, he focused his attentions on improving America's global reputation with the Iran Nuclear Deal, which was a groundbreaking move to thaw the relationship between Iran and the United States. However, this deal was later withdrawn by Donald Trump in 2018.

Could President Obama have done more to uplift African American communities more during his presidency? Would the following deaths have been prevented if Obama focused more on systemic racism instead of hoping things would improve naturally since an African American was given the top job? With him in power, the American presidency finally looked and felt different for eight years. His victory fulfilled a humungous achievement for the Civil Rights struggle by showcasing talented and extraordinary Black Americans who can excel at all facets of life. His wife, First Lady Michelle Obama, and two daughters, Sasha and Malia, also extended the image of Black American life by providing a conspicuous vision of a loving, healthy, and thriving African American family that defies racist stereotypes. However, was this really a sign of "Post-Racial" America? The harmonious afterglow did not fix the root causes of the nation's problems when it comes to racial conflicts. If anything, it all seemed repressed during Obama's presidency while the Republicans successfully gained more power over the years and exposed their racism more evidently.

Marissa Alexander's Miscarriage of Justice

When 31-year-old Marissa Alexander escaped domestic violence in 2012, she did not believe that she would be heading to prison herself. Alexander was at the house of her estranged husband, Rico Gray, when she received texts saying he was planning to kill her. This gave her enough reason to believe that her life was in danger. Although she tried to escape through the garage, the door did not open. Therefore, she retrieved her handgun and fired a "warning shot" towards Gray. The bullet smashed against the wall near Gray at head level, and then deflected into the ceiling. Nobody was injured by this warning shot, Alexander simply wanted to scare Gray enough to buy some time because her life was in imminent danger. This was purely a self-defense move, but a jury did not see it that way. The reason Alexander felt she could fire a warning shot was because of Florida's Stand Your Ground Law, which allows individuals to defend themselves using lethal force if they are trapped in a life-threatening situation. However, the law was not legal at the time Alexander tried to protect herself. Despite her evident history of being a domestic violence victim at the hands of her estranged husband, she was rejected self-defense immunity.

Angela Corey, the State Attorney, met the defendant and offered her a three-year plea deal, but Alexander took her case to trial because she had done nothing wrong except try to save her life, and nobody was injured by the bullet. The jury took only 12 minutes to convict her, and she received a 20-year prison sentence, which was mind-boggling. In 2013, the appellate court ordered a fresh trial when they discovered that the jury instructions during Alexander's case impermissibly shifted the burden of proof onto her when everybody else is innocent until proven guilty according to law. She was released on bail and put on house arrest. Corey refused to back down and aimed to prosecute Alexander for three consecutive 20-year sentences, that would have totaled 60 years if Alexander was proven guilty during the second trial. Democratic Florida Congresswoman, Corrine Brown, argued that Corey overcharged Alexander because of institutional racism. The National Organization for Women (NOW) petitioned Corey's removal from the case stating that Corey was misusing her powers in office by endangering domestic violence survivors. Although Alexander was released from a Jacksonville prison under a plea deal in 2015 that capped her sentence to the three years she had already served, she still had to go through all that unnecessary suffering while her name was dragged through the mud. Her life was destroyed because a White prosecutor did not view her as an equal who deserved proper justice.

The Shooting of Trayvon Martin

On February 26, 2012, Trayvon Martin was an African American teenage boy walking home from a quick trip to the convenience store. He was dressed in a hoodie and carrying a can of Arizona Iced Tea and Skittles when Zimmerman, a 28-year-old insurance-fraud investigator and neighborhood-watch volunteer captain, spotted him. Zimmerman called Sanford police to report that Martin appeared "suspicious" and then ignored the dispatcher's advice telling him not to approach the teenager. Moments after, he shot Martin dead and claimed that it was an act of self-defense. Protests were held for the Million Hoodie March in many cities because everyone believed Zimmerman profiled and killed Martin due to racial hatred. This prompted President Obama to say, "If I had a son, he would look like Trayvon." The murder raised the national debate about the controversial Stand Your Ground law in Florida, especially when people can use lethal weapons without hesitation if they simply do not like an innocent victim based on their skin color. Zimmerman was a wannabe cop who profiled Martin and chased him down before fatally shooting him and should not have been allowed to claim self-defense when he ignored the dispatcher's advice. Marissa Alexander was sentenced to 20 years in a Florida prison despite harming no one, while Zimmerman used the Stand Your Ground law in the same state to claim self-defense and was found "not guilty" on July 13, mere months after murdering Martin. Martin's death forced Sanford to announce new rules in November 2013, where volunteers of neighbor-hood watch can no longer carry guns while pursuing suspects.

The Unwarranted Killing of Philando Castile

On July 6, 2013, a routine traffic stop turned into an unfair execution for a mortally wounded Philando Castile. With his gun buried deep in his pocket, his last words on earth were, "I wasn't reaching for it." Jeronimo Yanez, a Minnesota cop, unexpectedly screamed and fired seven shots during a friendly conversation with Castile, who was only 32. The African American victim was still strapped in the car with his seatbelt on. John Choi, County Attorney, said, "No reasonable officer, knowing, seeing and hearing what Officer Yanez did at the time, would have used deadly force under these circumstances." Castile's murder caused a national fury when his girlfriend, Diamond Reynolds, posted a video of his shooting on Facebook. The video showed the victim bleeding to death right next to her in the vehicle. Even though Castile's family requested a murder charge, the officer was only given a count of manslaughter. Yanez claimed that Castile's "wide-set nose" possibly linked him to a convenience store robbery days before the shooting, but this was a poor attempt to sugarcoat that he murdered a man. Castile deserved the chance to be proven innocent before being executed by an unhinged cop during a traffic stop.

The Emergence of Black Lives Matter

In July 2013, a social movement using the hashtag #BlackLivesMatter emerged on social media 17 months after Trayvon Martin's death when his shooter, George Zimmerman, was acquitted. The movement quickly gained recognition while calling for nationwide protests following the deaths of Michael Brown in Missouri and Eric Garner in New York City. Although the originators of the hashtag and call to action, Patrisse Cullors, Opal Tomedi, and Alicia Garza, expanded the movement to a national network of over thirty local chapters over two years, Black Lives Matter is a decentralized network of activists, and there is no formal hierarchy. Their primary call to action is protection against police brutality and all racially motivated violence against Black people, especially when there is more than enough evidence to suggest that the law is not on the police's side. The movement further gained support through national and international headlines and took precedence after George Floyd's death in May 2020. It is estimated that around 15 to 26 million people currently participate in the movement, despite not being official "members" of the organization. In 2020, BLM is one of the most significant demonstrations in the history of the United States. They outspokenly advocate to defund the police and invest resources in Black communities. A Pew Research Center poll conducted in June 2020 discovered that most Americans across all racial and ethnic groups express their support for the Black Lives Matter movement.

The Killing of Eric Garner

Eric Garner was murdered on July 17, 2014, on a Staten Island sidewalk. The 43-year-old echoed the same last words as George Floyd when he died, saying, "I can't breathe." His only "crime" was selling loose cigarettes on the street. The police at the scene used the same deadly chokehold that killed both Garner and Floyd. Garner's mother, Gwen Carr, said, "George Floyd used the same words my son said six years ago. And now the cry is 'I can't breathe' again." After a lengthy legal process that frustrated the nation, none of the officers involved in his death were convicted. Daniel Pantaleo, the officer who conducted the chokehold on Garner, was fired after federal authorities passed civil rights charges against him. However, this was not sufficient punishment for murder. NYPD Sergeant Kizzy Adonis was only docked for 20 vacation days for her failure to supervise the situation, and the other half-dozen cops at the scene are still working on the force. There were no consequences for their brutal actions, which led to the death of an innocent man. Whether selling cigarettes is a crime or not, no one deserves to be executed by the police without a fair trial. Carr believed that the country reached a tipping point after Floyd's 2020 death, a mere 1200 miles away from where her son died. She said, "The world saw how long we have been treated this way, back to when my son was killed and even before that."

The Shooting of Michael Brown

Michael Brown was a caring and gentle 18-year-old unfairly portrayed in court documents as a suspect in a convenience store robbery. He was accused of assaulting the police officer who murdered him in August 2014. Weeks before his death, he left secondary school and planned to study to become a heating and cooling technician. Like any other teenager, he enjoyed playing video games and spending time with family and friends. His loved ones called him "Big Mike" or "Mike" because of his 1.9-meter frame that made him look like a gentle giant. His neighbors described him as a respectful boy who always listened to his grand-mother when she told him to go upstairs and never bothered anyone. However, the New York Times unfairly described Brown as "no angel," as though they were trying to say he deserved being killed. The comment sparked a lot of anger across social media because he was as normal as any other teenager. He occasionally smoked and drank alcohol, but those are not crimes anybody deserves the death penalty for. On the 9th of August, he allegedly stole a pack of cigarillos from a store, and offi-cer Darren Wilson shot him six times in the head and right arm. Brown's body remained on the street for four hours in his pool of blood before it was taken away. He was due to start studying at his new school the following Monday. Brown's mother, Lesley McSpadden, said that the family never got time to celebrate her son's departure for school and had to organize his funeral. A grand jury decided not to charge Wilson for murdering Brown.

The Shooting of Walter Scott

Walter Scott was a 50-year-old unarmed man facing away from a white po-lice officer when he was fatally shot at least eight times in North Charles-ton, South Carolina. All he did was attempt to flee away from the police to save his life, but that did not stop officer Michael Slager from repeat-edly gunning down the man even though he never presented any threat. Slager was forced to plead guilty by admitting that he did not shoot in self-defense, especially when a video of the killing recorded by a bystand-er was handed to the authorities. Unfortunately, this was not enough for the jury to be convinced of Slager's wrongdoing. It took almost a year for the high-profile case to result in a murder charge and much longer for an actual conviction. This proved that prosecutions against police officers are rare when it comes to racially motivated shootings.

The Death of Freddie Gray

On April 12th, 2015, Freddie Gray was a 25-year-old Black man from Baltimore arrested for possession of a "switchblade" that he did not use to harm anyone. Even though Gray's knife was not an illegal switchblade under Maryland law, he was still shoved inside a Baltimore Police Department van and was found unresponsive 45 minutes later with his spinal cord practically severed. After being in a coma for a week, he succumbed to his injuries on April 19th. A video of his arrest showed him screaming in agony, which prompted protests to demand the truth about what happened to Gray. A two-week investigation revealed that Gray's injuries occurred during the van's route, which involved six stops, including a passenger pick-up and two prisoner checks. On May 1st, 2015, State Attorney Marilyn Mosby stood in front of Baltimore's City Hall to announce criminal charges against the six offending police officers. However, the next two years proved to be a defeat for the prosecution. Five officers charged with Gray's murder are suing Mosby, claiming that Gray's arrest was justified. This showcased the Supreme Court precedent that allows police officers to make numerous mistakes in judgment while interpreting the law, if they are "reasonable." Gray's arrest for the so-called "switchblade" was classified as a "reasonable misunderstanding," and this led to his unfair execution because the police made a mistake.

The Death of Sandra Bland

Sandra Bland was a 28-year-old African American woman who died in police custody in south-east Texas in July 2015. Bland was pulled over in traffic by a former state trooper, Brian Encinia, for allegedly failing to indicate while she was switching lanes. Encinia aggressively pulled out his Taser on Bland, shouting, "Get out of the car! I will light you up. Get out!" When Bland cooperatively exited the vehicle, he ordered her on to the sidewalk while still pointing the Taser.

Three days after her arrest, she was found hanging in her cell at the Waller County Jail. Even though her death was ultimately ruled as suicide, her family remained suspicious of the circumstances. Unexpectedly, a video unearthed, which showed Bland's viewpoint during the arrest. The Bland family lawyer, Cannon Lambert, claimed that he did not see the footage before settling the lawsuit despite it being released as part of the legal discovery process. Texas Democrat representative, Garnet Coleman, expressed, "It is troubling that a crucial piece of evidence was withheld from Sandra Bland's family and legal team in their pursuit of justice." Encinia was never charged with murder despite the video evidence. After the incident, he was fired and briefly indicted for perjury for falsely claiming that he feared for his safety while arresting Bland. All charges against him were dropped after he agreed to never work as a police officer again.

The Shooting of Korryn Gaines

On August 1, 2016, cops from the Baltimore County Police Department arrived at a Randallstown apartment to serve warrants to Korryn Gaines, and her fiancé, Kareem Courtney. After a six-hour standoff, Gaines was fatally shot by the police officers even though they were only there to serve a warrant because she missed a court appearance for traffic-related charges. In comparison, Courtney's warrant was related to a domestic violence assault charge set in motion by Gaines. Police claimed that Gaines allegedly pointed a gun at them and that is why they fatally shot her, while also injuring her 5-year-old son who watched his mother's death. The jury initially awarded her family $38 million during a wrongful death lawsuit. However, this was later overturned by a Baltimore County Circuit Court judge who cited "Qualified Immunity" that protects police officers from liabilities while carrying out their duties. After it was determined that the judge made the wrong decision, the ruling was reinstated, and the family was finally awarded the money in a civil suit. The Gaines' family attorney, J. Wyndal Gordon, said, "Korryn Gaines died a horrible, tragic, sadistic death, and we just wanted justice for her and her family."

Kneeling for The Star-Spangled Banner

Colin Kaepernick, the former San Francisco 49ers quarterback, dove into controversy in 2016 by kneeling for the national anthem and refusing to stand up. He did so to peacefully protest police brutality, systemic racial injustice, and all the wrongdoings inflicted upon African Americans and minorities in the country. Kaepernick told NFL Media, "I am not going to stand up to show pride in a flag for a country that oppresses Black people and people of color. To me, this is bigger than football, and it would be selfish on my part to look the other way. There are bodies in the street and people getting paid leave and getting away with murder."

Although there was a public outcry over his actions because some people felt that he disrespected the anthem, the Niners coach, Chip Kelly, defended him, saying, "It is not my right to tell him not to do something. It is his right as a citizen." NFL Media also stated, "Players are encouraged but not required to stand during the playing of the national anthem." Kaepernick was aware that his kneel did not sit well with many people, especially since he did not seek permission or inform anyone in the club or team beforehand. He said, "This is not something that I am going to run by anybody. I am not looking for approval. I have to stand up for people that are oppressed. If they take my football away, my endorsements from me, I know that I stood up for what is right." When he was booed throughout the game by fans for supposedly disrespecting the flag, Kaepernick said, "Once again, I'm not anti-American. I love America. I love people. That is why I am doing this. I want to help make America better."

Despite his words showing true character with a lot of heart and compassion to stand for what is right, President Trump expressed rage for his kneeling during the anthem by calling him a "son of a b****." Trump also instructed Vice President Mike Pence to walk out of any games if players protested during the anthem. He famously tweeted on September 23rd, 2017, "If a player wants the privilege of making millions of dollars in the NFL, or other leagues, he or she should not be allowed to disrespect our Great American Flag (or Country) and should stand for the National Anthem. If not, YOU'RE FIRED. Find something else to do!" Many republicans were recording videos and taking photos of themselves burning Nike merchandise because the brand stood by Kaepernick's kneel. However, he continued being the voice of the company and was featured in an ad campaign that gathered both praise and criticism. In the award-winning Nike ad "Dream Crazy," Kaepernick said, "Believe in something, even if it means sacrificing everything."

The Man Whose Racism Divided the Country Beyond Belief

Donald Trump defied all expectations from the beginning of his campaign until he finally won the election in 2016 as the 45th President of the United States. Few people believed that he would run the whole nine yards, let alone win the election. Nobody imagined him succeeding in the primaries and gradually climbing through the polls. Everybody laughed him off during debates as they comfortably sat back and waited for Hillary Clinton to claim the top job. After all, she was an experienced and successful politician while he was a reality TV star with a shady business background. Americans did not need a billionaire in charge. Did they?

The Age of Trump

The Democrats relied heavily on Clinton's blue firewall, which was her strength in the Midwest. Those states have always been Democrats for decades. No one expected them to flip to the other side the way they did during the baffling 2016 Presidential election. These were working-class voters, predominantly white and without a college education, who had deserted the Democrat party in droves to adopt red MAGA (Make America Great Again) caps instead. These rural voters headed to the polls in large numbers because they felt overlooked and ignored by the establishment, especially by the coastal elite who were too busy enriching themselves. The Trump wave hit many communities hard, even though he made several derogatory comments both in public and private, showing a lack of moral compass. He picked a fight with Fox News' top presenter, Megyn Kelly, insulted decorated war veteran John McCain, mocked the weight of a Hispanic beauty pageant winner, and half-heartedly apologized when a secret video leaked showing him boast about making unwanted sexual advances towards women. Despite this outrageous and unprofessional behavior, he still climbed the polls, and the Republicans backed him with all their might. This showed the world that Trump's appeal and personality are much stronger than they thought. And back in 2016, he was bulletproof.

Trump held massive rallies instead of focusing on traditional door-knocking operations. He made an effort to travel to states, such as Michigan and Wisconsin, that were usually out of reach or uncared for. The budget for his campaign far exceeded Clinton's, in part because she had not been the one to spend money manufacturing MAGA hats. His campaign was the most unconventional that the world had ever seen, but this did not stop him and his family from having the last laugh from inside the White House. Since he won the election in 2016, he has consistently targeted minorities while empowering white supremacists. In the wake of George Floyd's murder, Trump did not show support for pro-testors. He called them "looters," and tried to shift the narrative away by claiming that more White people suffer from police brutality. He tried to find excuses for the actions of corrupt members of police departments across the nation instead of focusing on preventing the number of deaths regardless of race. Although police departments are not forced to report comprehensive data on killings during arrests, researchers compiled sta-tistics to reveal that Black Americans are more likely to meet their demise at the hands of law enforcement over White people.

Now in 2020, the United States is experiencing a seismic shift in the numbers of Americans admitting that racism is a pervasive problem and that police brutality can no longer go unchecked. People are marching down the streets and showing support for the Black Lives Matter move-ment. They are pleading for a wave of reforms to law enforcement, which should involve disbanding police departments and defunding forces across the nation. Instead of offering specific policy proposals to show support for substantive policing reforms, Trump responded on Twitter condemning calls to defund the police while attacking Democrats. On June 8, 2020, he tweeted, "This year has seen the lowest crime numbers in our Country's recorded history, and now the Radical Left Democrats want to Defund and Abandon our Police. Sorry, I want LAW & ORDER." According to Business Insider, "President Donald Trump's favorite words are 'strong' and 'powerful.' As president, it has become even more clear the words make up his measure of leadership. It's why he admires dic-tators and authoritarians, and why he has long encouraged US law enforcement to not worry so much about namby-pamby civil liberties and just get on with the business of letting the people know who's boss." This statement explains Trump's use of federal agents to police the streets of Portland while threatening to do the same in Milwaukee, Chicago, and any other city he deems is run by "Leftist Democrats."

Portland saw the worst of Trump's wrath and his secret police force. The unnerving presence of federal agents without badges arresting people in unmarked vans and deploying rubber bullets and tear gas on peaceful protestors is a severe violation of the First Amendment. While the people of these cities begged to defund the police to limit corruption, Trump militarized law enforcement instead by handing them weapons of war to feel like hardcore warriors rather than guardians of society. He supported Border Patrol by sticking to his promise of lifting their restrictions, which is the opposite of forbidding excessive force and ensuring due process. In turn, they became the warriors he needed to prevent peaceful protesters from exercising their freedom of speech, even though he defended white supremacists in Charlottesville for doing the exact same. As Democrats race to trample this violent strategy, Trump is attempting to secure a second term win by upending the United States Postal Service in Democrat areas right before millions of Americans are expected to vote by mail instead of in-person this November because of COVID-19. Despite voting by mail himself, he insisted that people avoid USPS services because it leads to voter fraud. A series of changes took place since June where iconic blue mailboxes were transported away on trucks, coupled with Trump's rants against mail-in voting, which fueled concerns that the Trump administration is interfering with the Postal Service to disrupt the election. The Postmaster General of USPS, who ordered this unnecessary interference, Louis DeJoy, was appointed by a Board of Governors made up of six members all chosen by Trump, and this is what makes the crisis so critically dangerous with the 2020 elections just around the corner.

The Death of Heather Heyer

On August 11, 2017, white nationalists took on Market Street Park, forcing Virginia State Police to declare it an unlawful gathering. This "Unite the Right" rally resulted from intense debate in Charlottesville over whether Robert E. Lee's statue should be taken down or not. Heyer was an activist who was fatally injured when 20-year-old James Alex Fields Jr deliberately drove his car into a crowd of peaceful protestors who stood against the white nationalists. He was convicted of first-degree murder, hit-and-run, and eight counts of malicious wounding with a final sentence of life in prison starting from July 2019. This hate crime showed the world how dangerous the far right was becoming, especially when empowered by Trump's support. He called the Charlottesville nationalists "very fine people." Heyer's final Facebook post said, "If you are not outraged, you are not paying attention." Her mother told the Huffington Post, "Heather was about stopping hatred. She was there with her friends trying to cross the street when the movement was breaking up that day. That is when she was ploughed down by a young driver who was intent on spreading hate and thought that his violent actions would fix the world." Heyer was described by her manager as a very opinionated woman who opposed Donald Trump and Jason Kessler, who was the organizer of the Unite the Right rally. He said, "She would literally sit in the office and cry at times because she was worried about what was going to happen to the country."

The Murder of Botham Jean

Botham Jean was fatally shot in his own apartment on September 6, 2018. When Amber Guyger used her key for the wrong apartment door at the South Side Flats apartment complex in Detroit, she set off a tragic chain of events that cost an innocent man his life, while also ending her career as a police officer. Guyger gunned down Botham Jean when she accidentally thought he was in the wrong apartment, only to later realize that hers was one floor below. Although prosecutors requested that the jury give her the maximum sentence, Guyger's defense attorneys argued that she made a "reasonable mistake" because she believed that she faced an intruder in her own home, and that "forced" her to fire her gun as "self-defense." Jean was simply sitting in his own apartment and eating ice cream before being murdered by a deranged cop. He was also shot directly in the chest, which meant that he had no chance of survival. It is also shocking that after killing Jean, Guyger's initial thought was that she would lose her job instead of focusing on the murder that would land her in jail for the pain she caused his loved ones. Her job security should have been the least of her problems at that moment. She gave Jean no opportunity for de-escalation or time to surrender before opening fire. Jean's uncle, Ignatius Jean, said, "The sound of gunshots did not have the resonance to be heard on our small island, but their impact was of nuclear proportions. A nuke had been unleashed on our family by someone charged to protect and serve." Guyger was sentenced to ten years in prison, and Jean's brother Brandt Jean expressed forgiveness by embracing her in the courtroom and suggesting that she find Christ.

The Killing of Ahmaud Arbery

When Ahmaud Arbery went for a jog on February 23, he was confronted by father and son, Gregory and Travis McMichael. As he entered a neighborhood called Santilla Shores, resident Gregory McMichael informed police that Arbery resembled a suspect supposedly responsible for a series of break-ins. The police were adamant there were no official reports filed about this alleged crime, but this did not prevent the McMichaels from arming themselves with a shotgun and pistol to pursue Arbery. As Arbery continued jogging, they followed him in their truck, saying, "Stop, stop, we want to talk to you." After they fired three shots, they claimed Arbery attacked Travis even though they were the ones following him with weapons while he was an unarmed jogger. It took over two months for the killer duo to be arrested along with the neighbor who recorded the video of this fatal encounter. The three men are currently in custody, but the case could not be convened due to COVID-19 restrictions. The delay in their formal murder charge is due to a fourth prosecutor turnover. Two local district attorneys had to remove themselves from the trial because of their personal and professional connections to Gregory McMichael. Despite the racial motive behind this killing, officials vehemently disagreed on whether the pair should be arrested. Jackie Johnson, Brunswick District Attorney, was accused by two county commissions for not letting police arrest the McMichaels directly after the murder took place. However, she denied the claim and placed the blame on prosecutors in her office, who supposedly prevented law enforcement officers from arresting the guilty pair.

Arbery was described by his family as a generous young man with a big heart. He enjoyed playing high school football and was about to turn 26 before his murder. The case went through so many hurdles, even though the shooters showed no remorse for their racist actions. This was because George McMichael is a former police detective with several law enforcement connections. Arbery's life was cut short because he dared to be a Black American going out for a jog.

The Shooting of Breonna Taylor

On March 13, 2020, Breonna Taylor, a 26-year-old emergency room technician, was brutally executed by law enforcement officers as she slept in her own bed. Around midnight, Louisville officers used a battering ram to break into her apartment while she and her boyfriend Kenneth Walker were in bed. When they heard the loud bang and woke up to confront what was going on, Walker initially fired his gun because he believed they were confronting burglars. That is when the police also fired numerous shots that struck Taylor. Walker told investigators that Taylor struggled for breath and coughed after being shot and was not given any medical attention for over twenty minutes. The police showed up there because they were investigating two other men who they believed were selling drugs from Taylor's home. The judge's order was a no-knock warrant that allowed law enforcement officials to break the door and enter without revealing their identity. No drugs were found at Taylor's home, but they had murdered an innocent woman who was asleep in the middle of the night.

Taylor's mother, Tamika Palmer, said that her daughter dreamed of a lifelong career in health care after serving as an EMT. She stated, "[Breonna] had a whole plan on becoming a nurse and buying a house and then starting a family. Breonna had her head on straight, and she was a very decent person. She did not deserve this. She was not that type of person."

The Louisville police claim they fired shots in Taylor's home after being fired upon first by her boyfriend. Walker expressed that he feared for his life and fired the shot in self-defense, thinking that somebody was breaking into their home in the middle of the night. He did not know these people were police officers because they did not announce their identity before breaking down the door. There were also multiple errors spotted in the police incident report that listed Taylor's injuries as "none," despite her being shot at least eight times. The report also falsely mentioned that officers did not force their way into the apartment, even though they used a battering ram to smash the door open. The Taylor family lawyer said, "The police had already located the main suspect in the investigation by the time they burst into the apartment. But they proceeded to spray gunfire into the residence with total disregard for the value of human life." There was also no body camera footage taken during the raid, which led to prosecutors dismissing the charges against those officers who were then ultimately allowed to walk free. The case was delayed due to the coronavirus pandemic, and city officials banned the use of no-knock warrants from June 11. It would have been Taylor's

27ᵗʰ birthday on June 5, and people used the hashtag #SayHerName to raise awareness. Democrat Senator Cory Booker tweeted, "Her life was tragically taken by police, and we will not stop marching for justice until it is served for her and her family. #SayHerName."

A Global Pandemic That "
Disrupted the Entire World

The United States has always been a beacon of strength and hope to the world, but its response to the COVID-19 pandemic has been uniquely hapless, undisciplined, ineffective, and selfish. The country handled the crisis poorly and accounts for 22% of all deaths, despite only being 4% of the world's population. A virus smaller than dust particles crippled the planet's most powerful nation, and America failed to protect its people, leaving them in financial ruin if they are lucky to escape death. The country lost its status as a global leader and careened between ineptitude and inaction. Despite all the warnings, the US squandered every opportunity to control and limit the spread. Although the nation benefits from considerable advantages, such as biomedical might and scientific expertise, it floundered it all way resulting in over 160,000 deaths as of August 2020. This was due to the sluggish response from the Trump administration, which placed more importance on the economy than healthcare and people's safety. Chronic underfunding of public health also neutered the country's ability to prevent the pathogen from destroying so many lives. Racist policies still in place since the days of slavery and colonization placed Black Americans and people of color at risk the most.

All those decades of shredding the nation's social safety net forced millions of low-paid workers to struggle for their livelihood with no end in sight. President Donald Trump repeatedly lied and downplayed the pandemic instead of preparing for the once-in-a-generation crisis. Back in February, he claimed that the virus would weaken by April when the weather is warmer, even though the World Health Organization stated that new aggressive strains can be transmitted in hot and humid areas. He stated that the virus would disappear one day, like a miracle, while ignoring experts warning that community-related cases will skyrocket. Trump also kept convincing people that the economy is more important than their lives. He claimed that an economic shutdown would cause far greater deaths than caused by COVID-19. At present, the White House estimates that up to 240,000 Americans could perish from the virus, while other experts say those numbers could be as high as 1.2 million. To deflect from his own mistakes, he suggested limiting the number of tests to keep the numbers down, and began promoting a controversial prescription drug "Hydroxychloriquine," as preventative treatment despite lacking evidence of its effectiveness. After rushing to open schools during a severe pandemic so workers can continue breaking backs for the economy, he also suggested ingesting disinfectant into the body. He said, "[…] and then I see the disinfectant where it knocks it out in a minute. One minute. And is there a way we can do something like that, by injection inside or almost a cleaning? So it'd be interesting to check that. I'm not a doctor. But I'm, like, a person that has a good you-know-what."

When Dr. Anthony Fauci, the country's top infectious disease expert, urged state and local leaders to be strict about enforcing mask rules for the public's protection, Trump vowed not to order Americans to wear masks. The president stated that people should be allowed "certain freedom," which led to a lot of public outbursts where "Karens" and "Kens" were filmed, causing commotions over being forced to wear a mask while shopping. These white women and men were made into memes and canceled for their absurdly problematic behavior, which led to the "Cancel Culture," also known as "Face the Consequences of Your Actions Culture." Most Karens and Kens were publicly called out for being anti-maskers during the pandemic since they believe masks are a threat to their freedom, especially since Trump emboldens them to not care about protecting others. They are also outspokenly racist, and a viral example of this is the woman who phoned the police on a Black man who was bird watching in Central Park. She purposely said during the call she felt threatened by an African American man, after implying prior to the call that she knew full well that she would be endangering his life in the wake of George Floyd's murder. Since Trump himself is not setting a good example by wearing a mask and motivating others to do the same, the world continues to see videos of people throwing tantrums in public because they feel that their liberty is being squashed by a piece of cloth.

The Killing of George Floyd

On May 25, 2020, Minneapolis police officers arrested a 46-year-old man named George Floyd after an employee from a convenience store claimed that Floyd purchased cigarettes using a counterfeit $20 bill. Only seventeen minutes had passed after the first squad car's arrival at the scene before Floyd was already pinned down by three officers and unconscious, eventually showing no signs of life. Combined videos filmed by bystanders revealed that Floyd begged officer Derek Chauvin to stop kneeling on his neck because he could not breathe before he went limp. The videos showed officers conducting a series of actions that violated all policies of the Minneapolis Police Department, leading to the death of a man who struggled to breathe. The officers also ignored onlookers who called out for help, and the day after Floyd's death, all four officers were fired. On May 29, Mike Freemen, the Hennepin County Attorney, announced second-degree manslaughter and third-degree murder charges against Derek Chauvin. Chauvin was the leading officer seen kneeling on Floyd's neck for at least eight minutes, sustaining this position even after Floyd had gone limp. On June 3, prosecutors added more severe charges of murder against Chauvin and then arrested the other officers as well for aiding and abetting second-degree murder. This incident sparked global protests during a once-in-a-generation pandemic. People could no longer remain silent and they took to the streets to support Black Lives Matter. Many also tried to dismiss the incident, especially a lawyer for Thomas Lane, who insisted that Floyd "killed himself" by overdosing on Fentanyl while having an underlying heart condition. Floyd's aunt, Angela Harrelson, and Uncle Selwyn Jones told the Star Tribune they were disappointed in this court filing that focused on Floyd's history of addiction rather than the actual cause of his death, which was police brutality. Jones said, "It is a sign of desperation.

I want to know when did police officers get their law degrees? When did they get voted into being judges, and when does four people do the job of a jury?"

In the wake of Floyd's unfair death at the hands of a white Minneapolis officer, demonstrations erupted across the country. Lawmakers in New York and many other states had to scramble fast to pass legislation that banned police chokeholds. Black Lives Matter social justice protests put pressure on communities and federal officials to consider law enforcement reforms and renew calls for racial equality. This led to plans of defunding and disbanding police, empowering civilian review boards, taking down Confederate symbols, and fostering inclusion by painting Black Lives Matter murals to show progress. However, a lot more needs to be done to undo centuries of systemic racism that led to this moment. Floyd's death went viral when the video of Chauvin kneeling on his neck was posted online, and this magnified the issues protesters are marching on the streets to address. Black Americans face glaring inequalities for housing, healthcare, food, security, jobs, and education. They also fear for their lives since any police officer can kill them with a vendetta. Demonstrators are also calling for reforms to outlaw voter suppression and to close the wealth gap. They are demanding government officials to invest money into poor communities towards quality education systems and provide access to affordable healthcare and housing.

Unfortunately, lawmakers have shielded themselves away from transformational and revolutionary steps to dismantle systemic racism. This applies to both Republicans and Democrats. During the Democratic National Convention, the campaign for the party's presidential nominee,

Joe Biden, said extraordinarily little about the reforms asked for by protesters risking their lives. Instead of defunding the police, Biden opposes cutting law enforcement resources and wants to allocate even more funds to community policing. He also chose Kamala Harris, a prosecutor, as his Vice President, and this was not the wisest move. Even though she is a person of color with a tremendous talent for the job, this was not the right time to promote and uplift cops on such a global scale when Americans are insisting that law enforcement be defunded immediately. President Donald Trump has also defended the police while calling Black Lives Matter a "symbol of hate." He also called protesters "terrorists," while white nationalists in Charlottesville were given his respect. Although the U.S. House of Representatives passed the George Floyd Justice in Policing Act, which bans police practices like chokeholds and no-knock warrants, it is not an aggressive enough move to prevent racial discrimination. In addition, what little good it could do is still in jeopardy, as the George Floyd Justice in Policing Act is still currently being held up in Senate and few expect it to pass. If it does, it then goes to the President, who must choose between approving the bill or vetoing it, where it returns to congress in an indefinite cycle that many bills do not survive. Rashad Robinson, the president of Color of Change and a civil rights advocacy group, said, "Divesting and downsizing police and increasing funding for poor communities is key to ending systemic racism within law enforcement. I think the movement has tremendous momentum right now, and what we are seeing is us running up against entrenched power that would like to put band-aids on things, so we go away. But the movement is very clear that we need structural change."

The President's Monumental Focus

On June 26, 2020, Donald Trump signed an executive order to protect monuments. He said, "I just had the privilege of signing a very strong Executive Order protecting American Monuments, Memorials, and Statues – and combatting recent Criminal Violence. Long prison terms for these lawless acts against our Great Country!" He authorized Federal Government to arrest anyone who is caught vandalizing or destroying any statue with up to 10 years in prison. This legislation moved surprisingly fast, considering that Breonna Taylor's shooters still have not been arrested yet. Trump focused more on preventing US statues from being pulled down than the murder of unarmed Black man George Floyd by police. The measure states, "Many of the rioters, arsonists, and left-wing extremists who have carried out and supported these acts have explicitly identified themselves with ideologies – such as Marxism – that call for the destruction of the United States system of government." He then accused protestors of possessing a profound ignorance of American history instead of acknowledging the reasons these monuments do not belong in the modern world and should be taken down. The Executive Order also reiterates that police departments who fail to guard statues from vandalism or damage will be defunded. Yet, they still will not suffer consequences for racially profiling and killing another victim. This prompted social justice activist, Shaun King, to tweet, "Statues of the white European they claim is Jesus should also come down. They are a form of white supremacy."

Epilogue

Despite what America has done to us, we will always remain resilient and united to fight and stand another day. No matter how many Black bodies they have tragically and unfairly stolen from our family and friends, we will always remain spirited and stronger than ever. We are America's unwanted guests forced to stand and watch other freedom seekers from around the world reap the benefits of our fruits and labor. This was snatched from our blood, sweat, and tears for 400 years. Yet, we are forced to view and adapt to the world through the eyes of our oppressors.

Enough is enough. You have beaten my body. You have raped my mother, sister, brother, uncle, and nieces, and this Stockholm Syndrome forced me to submit to your whims as I lived in fear of your wrath. Nothing is left for you to steal from me anymore. You have Jim Crowed me, segregated me, and castrated me. Meanwhile, my only fault was to seek liberty, justice, and peace.

"The most dangerous creation of any society is the man who has nothing to lose."

James Baldwin, The Fire Next Time

Derrick Newton

References

10 years since Oscar Grant's death: What happened at Fruitvale Station? SFChronicle.com. Retrieved 27 August 2020, from https://www.sf-chronicle.com/bayarea/article/10-years-since-Oscar-Grant-s-death-What-13489585.php.

A timeline of Colin Kaepernick kneeling in protest against police brutality. (2020). Retrieved 27 August 2020, from https://www.washingtonpost.com/sports/2020/06/01/colin-kaepernick-kneeling-history/.

America's Retirement Race Gap, and Ideas for Closing It. Nytimes.com. (2020). Retrieved 27 August 2020, from https://www.nytimes.com/2020/08/14/business/retirement-inequality-racism.html.

Bailey, A. (2020). *On this day four years ago, Colin Kaepernick began his peaceful protests during the national anthem.* The Milford Daily News. Retrieved 27 August 2020, from https://www.milforddailynews.com/news/20200826/on-this-day-four-years-ago-colin-kaepernick-began-his-peaceful-protests-during-national-anthem.

Bates, K. (2018). *A Look Back At Trayvon Martin's Death, And The Movement It Inspired.* Npr.org. Retrieved 4 July 2020, from https://www.npr.org/sections/codeswitch/2018/07/31/631897758/a-look-back-at-trayvon-martins-death-and-the-movement-it-inspired.

Black Lives Matter May Be the Largest Movement in U.S. History. Nytimes.com. (2020). Retrieved 11 August 2020, from https://www.nytimes.com/interactive/2020/07/03/us/george-floyd-protests-crowd-size.html.

Bloomberg - Are you a robot? Bloomberg.com. (2020). Retrieved 27 August 2020, from https://www.bloomberg.com/opinion/articles/2020-08-27/tracking-donald-trump-s-presidency-ahead-of-2020-election.

Brewer, J. (2020). *For Black athletes, social unrest is not a game, and this historic action is an urgent plea*. The Washington Post. Retrieved 24 August 2020, from https://www.washingtonpost.com/sports/2020/08/26/black-america-nba-strike/.

Bro, S. (2020). *My daughter Heather Heyer's death taught me how to grieve. We all need to know how today*. Fortune. Retrieved 13 August 2020, from https://fortune.com/2020/08/12/heather-heyer-charlottesville-anniversary-grief/.

Brooks, D. (2020). *The Culture of Policing Is Broken*. The Atlantic. Retrieved 9 July 2020, from https://www.theatlantic.com/ideas/archive/2020/06/how-police-brutality-gets-made/613030/.

Bult, L., & McShane, L. (2016). *Minnesota cop who killed Philando Castile could face up to 10 years on manslaughter charges*. Nydailynews.com. Retrieved 24 July 2020, from https://www.nydailynews.com/news/national/minnesota-charged-philando-castile-shooting-article-1.2875862.

Bydlak, J. (2020). *Opinion | Donald Trump Isn't Richard Nixon. He's Jimmy Carter*. POLITICO. Retrieved 15 August 2020, from https://www.politico.com/news/magazine/2020/08/24/not-nixon-trump-carter-comparison-400925.

Carvajal, N., Westwood, S., & Kelly, C. (2020). *Trump says he signed executive order to protect monuments*. CNN. Retrieved 22 August 2020, from https://edition.cnn.com/2020/06/26/politics/trump-signs-monuments-executive-order/index.html.

Cirilo, F. (2020). *Colorblindness has become a conservative shield for racial inequality*. The Washington Post. Retrieved 27 August 2020, from https://www.washingtonpost.com/outlook/2020/08/07/colorblindness-has-become-conservative-shield-racial-inequality/.

Clegg, L. (2019). *The Truth about America's Racist Presidents*. Portlandobserver.com. Retrieved 23 July 2020, from http://portlandobserver.com/news/2019/aug/14/truth-about-americas-racist-presidents/.

Chan, M. (2019). *Officer in Eric Garner Death Fired After NYPD Investigation. Here's What to Know About the Case*. Time. Retrieved 13 August 2020, from https://time.com/5642648/eric-garner-death-daniel-pantaleo-suspended/.

Coates, T. (2013). *Trayvon Martin and the Irony of American Justice*. The Atlantic. Retrieved 14 July 2020, from https://www.theatlantic.com/national/archive/2013/07/trayvon-martin-and-the-irony-of-american-justice/277782/.

Court filings: Medical examiner thought George Floyd had 'fatal level' of fentanyl in system. FOX 9 Minneapolis-St. Paul. (2020). Retrieved 27 August 2020, from https://www.fox9.com/news/court-filings-medical-examiner-thought-george-floyd-had-fatal-level-of-fentanyl-in-system.

Colin Kaepernick protests anthem over treatment of minorities. The Undefeated. (2020). Retrieved 27 August 2020, from https://theundefeated.com/features/colin-kaepernick-protests-anthem-over-treatment-of-minorities/.

Collins, S. (2020). *The killing of Ahmaud Arbery, an unarmed black jogger in Georgia, explained*. Vox. Retrieved 27 August 2020, from https://www.vox.com/identities/2020/5/6/21249202/ahmaud-arbery-jogger-killed-in-georgia-video-shooting-grand-jury.

Croft, J. (2017). *Philando Castile shooting: Dashcam video shows rapid event*. CNN. Retrieved 7 July 2020, from https://edition.cnn.com/2017/06/20/us/philando-castile-shooting-dashcam/index.html.

Cox, J., Bui, L., & Brown, D. (2015). *Who was Freddie Gray? How did he die? And what led to the mistrial in Baltimore?* The Washington Post. Retrieved 14 August 2020, from https://www.washingtonpost.com/local/who-was-freddie-gray-and-how-did-his-death-lead-to-a-mistrial-in-baltimore/2015/12/16/b08df7ce-a433-11e5-9c4e-be37f66848bb_story.html.

DeGregory, C. (2019). *deGregory: 'Sandra Bland did not kill herself' | The Atlanta Voice*. The Atlanta Voice | Atlanta GA News. Retrieved 15 August 2020, from https://www.theatlantavoice.com/articles/degregory-sandra-bland-op-ed/.

Dickson, E. (2019). *Man Who Killed Heather Heyer at Charlottesville Sentenced to Life in Prison, Plus 419 Years*. Rolling Stone. Retrieved 12 August 2020, from https://www.rollingstone.com/culture/culture-news/heather-heyer-james-fields-charlottesville-murderer-859182/.

Edelson, C. (2020). *How Donald Trump became the 'Showgirls' of presidents*. MarketWatch. Retrieved 27 August 2020, from https://www.marketwatch.com/story/how-donald-trump-became-the-showgirls-of-presidents-2020-08-25.

From Eric Garner's death to firing of NYPD officer: A timeline of key events. Usatoday.com. (2019). Retrieved 10 August 2020, from https://www.usatoday.com/story/news/2019/08/20/eric-garner-timeline-chokehold-death-daniel-pantaleo-fired/2059708001/.

Glanton, D. (2019). *Four years after her death, Sandra Bland gets to tell her side of the story.* chicagotribune.com. Retrieved 20 August 2020, from https://www.chicagotribune.com/columns/dahleen-glanton/ct-met-dahleen-glanton-sandra-bland-cellphone-video-20190510-story.html.

Graham, J. (2020). *5 reasons you might be underestimating Donald Trump.* Deseret News. Retrieved 27 August 2020, from https://www.deseret.com/indepth/2020/8/26/21372623/election-2020-democrats-might-be-underestimating-donald-trump-republicans-boat-parade.

Here's What You Need to Know About Breonna Taylor's Death. Nytimes.com. (2020). Retrieved 27 August 2020, from https://www.nytimes.com/article/breonna-taylor-police.html.

Hines, M. (2020). *Avowed neo-Nazi James Fields sentenced to life in prison for Charlottesville hate crimes.* Usatoday.com. Retrieved 19 August 2020, from https://www.usatoday.com/story/news/2019/06/28/james-fields-jr-charlottesville-sentencing-heather-heyer-unite-the-right/1587233001/.

Hills, M. (2020). *What has Trump achieved at half-way mark?* BBC News. Retrieved 27 August 2020, from https://www.bbc.com/news/world-us-canada-38663043.

Hitchcock, W. (2018). *The Age of Eisenhower: America and the World in the 1950s* (5th ed.). Simon & Schuster.

How George Floyd Was Killed in Police Custody. Nytimes.com. (2020). Retrieved 27 August 2020, from https://www.nytimes.com/2020/05/31/us/george-floyd-investigation.html.

Howard, J., & Rogers, K. (2020). *US racial inequality just as deadly as Covid-19 if not more, report suggests.* CNN. Retrieved 10 August 2020, from https://edition.cnn.com/2020/08/26/health/racial-inequality-death-rate-covid-19-wellness/index.html.

Hutchinson, B. (2019). *Death of an innocent man: Timeline of wrong-apartment murder trial of Amber Guyger.* ABC News. Retrieved 15 August 2020, from https://abcnews.go.com/US/death-innocent-man-timeline-wrong-apart-ment-murder-trial/story?id=65938727.

Jones, V. (2020). *Opinion: Why I walked away from Democrats to support President Trump*. CNN. Retrieved 27 August 2020, from https://edition.cnn.com/2020/08/25/opinions/why-support-trump-opinion-jones/index.html.

Joseph, P. (2016). *Racism During Barack Obama Presidency*. The Washington Post. Retrieved 12 August 2020, from https://www.washingtonpost.com/graphics/national/obama-legacy/racism-during-presidency.html.

Karni, A. (2020). *Donald Trump: Who He Is and What He Stands For*. Nytimes.com. Retrieved 14 August 2020, from https://www.nytimes.com/interactive/2020/us/elections/donald-trump.html.

Kilgore, E. (2020). *No, Uncle Joe, Trump Is Hardly Our First Racist President*. Intelligencer. Retrieved 27 August 2020, from https://nymag.com/intelligencer/2020/07/no-uncle-joe-trump-is-hardly-our-first-racist-president.html.

Lavietes, M., Lopez, O., & Wulfhorst, E. (2020). *'A pandemic in a pandemic': Coronavirus deepens racial gaps in America*. U.S. Retrieved 27 August 2020, from https://www.reuters.com/article/us-usa-race-money-insight/a-pandemic-in-a-pandemic-coronavirus-deepens-racial-gaps-in-america-idUSKBN25G1EW.

Lartey, J. (2020). *Why the officers who shot and killed Breonna Taylor may never be arrested*. the Guardian. Retrieved 27 August 2020, from https://www.theguardian.com/us-news/2020/aug/10/breonna-taylor-killing-officers-may-never-be-arrested.

Laughland, O. (2019). *Sandra Bland: video released nearly four years after death shows her view of arrest*. the Guardian. Retrieved 23 August 2020, from https://www.theguardian.com/us-news/2019/may/07/sandra-bland-video-footage-arrest-death-police-custody-latest-news.

Levin, S. (2019). *Officer punched Oscar Grant and lied about facts in 2009 killing, records show*. the Guardian. Retrieved 10 August 2020, from https://www.theguardian.com/us-news/2019/may/02/officer-punched-oscar-grant-and-lied-about-facts-in-2009-killing-records-show.

Li, D. (2019). *Colin Kaepernick reveals the specific police shooting that led him to kneel*. NBC News. Retrieved 13 August 2020, from https://www.nbcnews.com/news/us-news/colin-kaepernick-reveals-specific-police-shooting-led-him-kneel-n1044306.

Lopez, G. (2017). *Cleveland just fired the cop who shot and killed 12-year-old Tamir Rice more than 2 years ago*. Vox. Retrieved 20 August 2020, from https://www.vox.com/identities/2017/5/30/15713254/cleveland-police-tamir-rice-timothy-loehmann.

Lopez, G. (2017). *Ex-cop Michael Slager sentenced to 20 years in prison for killing unarmed black man*. Vox. Retrieved 12 August 2020, from https://www.vox.com/2015/4/8/8368197/walter-scott-police-shooting.

Mahbubani, R. (2020). *The full story of how the Ahmaud Arbery 'lynching' became a national flashpoint for justice*. Insider. Retrieved 12 August 2020, from https://www.insider.com/ahmaud-arbery-shooting-killed-jogging-travis-gregory-mcmichael-georgia-justice-2020-5.

Marketing, C. (2020). *Understanding Systemic Racism*. Eisenhower Public Library. Retrieved 27 August 2020, from https://eisenhowerlibrary.org/understanding-systemic-racism/.

McVeigh, K. (2012). *Trayvon Martin's death: the story so far*. the Guardian. Retrieved 28 July 2020, from https://www.theguardian.com/world/2012/mar/20/trayvon-martin-death-story-so-far.

NY officer fired over 'I can't breathe' death. BBC News. (2019). Retrieved 12 August 2020, from https://www.bbc.com/news/world-us-canada-49399302.

O'Donovan, B. (2020). *Will Donald Trump get a second season as president?* RTE.ie. Retrieved 27 August 2020, from https://www.rte.ie/news/analysis-and-comment/2020/0827/1161628-donald-trump-tv-president/.

Officer won't be charged for killing Michael Brown. BBC News. (2020). Retrieved 31 July 2020, from https://www.bbc.com/news/world-us-canada-53603923.

O'Kruk, A. (2020). *A Look at Police Brutality in America*. NBC Boston. Retrieved 22 July 2020, from https://www.nbcboston.com/news/national-international/a-look-at-police-brutality-in-america/2152297/.

Oprysko, C. (2020). *George W. Bush laments 'shocking failure' in treatment of black Americans*. POLITICO. Retrieved 8 August 2020, from https://www.politico.com/news/2020/06/02/george-w-bush-protest-297133.

Page, S. (2020). *Even as president, Donald Trump takes a familiar stance: The political outsider*. Usatoday.com. Retrieved 27 August 2020, from https://

www.usatoday.com/story/news/politics/elections/2020/08/27/trump-speaks-rnc-white-house-rally-support-base/3441526001/.

Panetta, G. (2020). *Larry Kudlow argues systemic racism doesn't exist because Barack Obama won '79 million white votes' in his 2 presidential runs*. Business Insider. Retrieved 21 July 2020, from https://www.businessinsider.com/kudlow-systemic-racism-isnt-real-because-obama-won-79-million-white-votes-2020-6.

Peoples, L. (2017). *She Went to Prison for Firing a Warning Shot at Her Abuser. Now She's Free*. The Cut. Retrieved 17 July 2020, from https://www.thecut.com/2017/03/marissa-alexander-case-stand-your-ground-florida.html.

Pilkington, E. (2020). *Will justice finally be done for Emmett Till? Family hope a 65-year wait may soon be over*. the Guardian. Retrieved 17 August 2020, from https://www.theguardian.com/us-news/2020/apr/25/emmett-till-long-wait-for-justice.

Prosecutor: No charges for officer in Michael Brown's death. POLITICO. (2020). Retrieved 19 August 2020, from https://www.politico.com/news/2020/07/30/no-charges-michael-brown-death-388968.

Prudente, T. (2020). *Appeals court finds judge erred in wiping out $38 million verdict over police shooting of Korryn Gaines*. Baltimoresun.com. Retrieved 16 August 2020, from https://www.baltimoresun.com/news/crime/bs-md-cr-korryn-gaines-verdict-reinstated-20200701-joywm-4ravzcy3pu4k3d24i6rku-story.html.

Rice, S. (2020). *My 12-year-old son, Tamir Rice, was killed by police. I'm not allowed to be normal*. ABC News. Retrieved 23 August 2020, from https://abcnews.go.com/GMA/News/12-year-son-tamir-rice-killed-police-im/story?id=71654873.

Rodgers, W. (2020). *Changing the Federal Reserve mandate could provide a down payment to ending racial inequality*. The Conversation. Retrieved 19 August 2020, from https://theconversation.com/changing-the-federal-reserve-mandate-could-provide-a-down-payment-to-ending-racial-inequality-144102.

Salinger, T. (2016). *Fatal shooting of Korryn Gaines by Maryland police officer 'justified,' prosecutors say*. Nydailynews.com. Retrieved 14 August 2020, from https://www.nydailynews.com/news/crime/fatal-shooting-korryn-gaines-justified-prosecutors-article-1.2801015.

Scott Glover, C. (2020). *A key miscalculation by officers contributed to the tragic death of Breonna Taylor*. CNN. Retrieved 27 August 2020, from https://edition.cnn.com/2020/07/23/us/breonna-taylor-police-shooting-invs/index.html.

Schuppe, J. (2017). *Florida mom convicted of shooting at husband wants stronger stand your ground law*. NBC News. Retrieved 11 July 2020, from https://www.nbcnews.com/news/us-news/woman-who-lost-stand-your-ground-case-wants-law-strengthened-n737191.

Spells, A., & Levenson, E. (2020). *Protesters gather outside Ferguson Police Department on anniversary of Michael Brown's death*. CNN. Retrieved 16 August 2020, from https://edition.cnn.com/2020/08/10/us/ferguson-protests-michael-brown/index.html.

The struggle for civil rights | Miller Center. Miller Center. Retrieved 27 August 2020, from https://millercenter.org/the-presidency/educational-resources/age-of-eisenhower/struggle-civil-rights.

The last 30 minutes of George Floyd's life. BBC News. (2020). Retrieved 27 August 2020, from https://www.bbc.com/news/world-us-canada-52861726.

The Murder of Emmett Till | American Experience | PBS. Pbs.org. Retrieved 10 August 2020, from https://www.pbs.org/wgbh/americanexperience/features/till-timeline/.

Tyson, T. (2017). *The Blood of Emmett Till* (12th ed.). Simon & Schuster.

Vann, M., & Ortiz, E. (2017). *Ex-police officer who fatally shot Walter Scott gets 20-year prison sentence*. NBC News. Retrieved 9 August 2020, from https://www.nbcnews.com/storyline/walter-scott-shooting/walter-scott-shooting-michael-slager-ex-officer-sentenced-20-years-n825006.

Vera, A., & Joseph, E. (2019). *Maryland judge overturns $37 million awarded to family of woman killed in police standoff*. CNN. Retrieved 11 August 2020, from https://edition.cnn.com/2019/02/16/us/baltimore-judge-overturns-korryn-gaines-shooting-verdict/index.html.

Westbrook, L. (2014). *Tamir Rice shot 'within two seconds'*. BBC News. Retrieved 27 June 2020, from https://www.bbc.com/news/av/world-us-canada-30220700.

www.ingramcontent.com/pod-product-compliance
Lightning Source LLC
Chambersburg PA
CBHW051348150726
48000CB00003B/1100